To Bee or Not To Bee

*A book for beeings who feel there's more
to life than just making honey*

by John Penberthy

Sound Publishing

Preface

When Buzz Bee first introduced himself to me, I could hardly believe it. I'm just your everyday, average person; not the kind who gets mystical inspirations on any kind of a regular basis. But there he was saying, "Here are the first six chapters — write." Now I knew the real reason for buying my word processor four months earlier.

As I emerged from my meditation, I mentioned it to Peggy. "You know all these ideas I've been having about writing an article relating bees and people? Well, it just came to me that it's supposed to be a story, a book. The first six chapters just came to me from nowhere."

Nowhere? As I began the daily routine of sitting down at the word processor, I began to wonder exactly where all this stuff was coming from. Thirty, forty minutes would pass without my being aware of anything but the next line on the screen. When I'd finally stop and lean back in my chair to see what I'd written, I was astounded. Something extraordinary was going on.

Best of all was the satisfaction, the fulfillment. Sometimes after reading a just-written page, I'd scream a guttural "Yeaaah!" at the top of my lungs. For the first time in my adult life, I was 100 percent me. Not 98 or 99; 100 percent.

What is it about this connection with our unique purpose that is so fulfilling? Although we've all experienced glimpses of it, somehow other things seem to get in the way — job, family, responsibilities. But only if we let them.

To Bee or Not To Bee is the story of Buzz's search for his true purpose. It's an adventure beyond his wildest imagination which confronts him with some of life's most important lessons. More often than not, he's pulled through them dragging and kicking, and always before he thinks he's ready. Sound familiar? If so, maybe, in a way, it's your story too.

John Penberthy

Copyright ©1987 by John Penberthy

All rights reserved. No part of this book may be reproduced in any form or by any means without the prior written consent of the publisher, excepting brief quotes used in connection with reviews written specifically for inclusion in magazines or newspapers.

Published by: Sound Publishing
2929 East Seventh Avenue
Denver, Colorado 80206

Printed in the United States of America

Library of Congress Catalogue Number: 87-080850

ISBN: 0-911777-15-6

To Peggy, who believed in me.

And to Sai Baba, who blew my mind.

It was just the kind of day Buzz Bee loved most — warm in the sunlight and cool in the shadows. The earth was still damp from the previous afternoon's thunderstorm, and the clover was exquisitely succulent. Dandelion yellow speckled the lush green meadow in every direction, with poppy orange thrown in for good measure. It contrasted with the deep blue sky in a way that pleased Buzz beyond words.

The air hummed with the sound of honeybees — bees scouring the meadow for just the right blossom, bees dipping into flowers for their nectar and pollen, and bees returning to the hive laden with their sweet bounty. It was a very industrious scene, Buzz thought, if you stopped to think about it.

As he observed the activity around him, Buzz's mind drifted off into that secret, other-worldly place it loved to explore. Although his eyes were open, the scene before him gradually faded from Buzz's reality. Why did anything exist?....How did it happen?....Why were they here?....What was the point of it all?....Who was he, really?....

A passing worker jolted him back to the task at hand. "Let's go, Buzz; there's work to do."

He instinctively dipped into the dandelion he stood on, and began probing for nectar. But as he did, he thought, "Here we go again. What's the big rush? This is a beautiful valley we live in, yet no one seems at all interested in anything except working to expand the colony." It already supported 31,000 bees. Buzz didn't see why it was so important for it to keep on growing.

When he could hold no more nectar, Buzz moved to another flower and began collecting pollen. Grain by grain he pulled it from the stamen, wadded it into a tight yellow ball and carefully fastened it to the stiff hairs on the back of his right rear leg. Then he meticulously formed another wad of pollen, attaching it to his left rear leg. As he lifted off for the hive, Buzz flew extra hard to compensate for his heavy load.

He landed at the entrance and made his way toward the honeycomb. As always, the passageways were a chaotic maze of bees moving every which-way, constantly bumping into one another. And the darkness didn't help matters any. "Surely there must bee a better way," Buzz thought, as he carefully picked his way through the throng.

Apparently he wasn't moving fast enough, for he heard a comment from out of the swarm, "Move it, Buzz; you're holding us all up." Then, in his hurry to get to the honeycomb, he bumped into another bee and spilled his pollen. "If you can't do something right, don't do it at all," growled the voice behind him.

Embarrassed, Buzz quickly collected the spilled pollen and hurriedly made his way to the honeycomb. He regurgitated his nectar into a honey cell as other workers removed his pollen wads and deposited them into a pollen cell, tamping them down tightly. Not a second was wasted. Buzz always felt tense inside the hive, but for some reason today was intolerable. He couldn't wait to get back outside and tried to hurry to the entrance, but it was useless fighting the confusion. It seemed an eternity before he finally saw the welcome slit of daylight piercing the entrance.

Buzz took off for the meadow, but stopped on an aspen twig at its edge to regain his composure. Was there something wrong with him? Why couldn't he just bee content working all the time like the other bees? Why couldn't they understand that there was more to life than building the hive and raising the brood?

Buzz knew he was as good a worker as any in the colony. Yet today something was really bothering him, and it was affecting his performance. He was already getting a reputation as an eccentric, what with his weird questions and all. Now he was starting to look lazy and incompetent as well.

He surveyed the meadow, the valley and the mountains beyond. Yes, he knew this was the only meadow in the valley, and a small one at that. He knew that the colony was totally dependent on the clover and flowers that grew there. And he knew that they were in continual competition with the bumblebees, hummingbirds and butterflies for its limited supply. If he'd heard it once, he'd heard the queen say it a thousand times: "Workers, we have only a small meadow to support us, so let's work extra hard and keep the honeycomb topped off all day long."

Although he was getting tired of the same old routine day after day, it was the subtle fear Buzz sensed throughout the colony that troubled him the most. It was an unspoken, yet driving force that seemed to rob them of life. Although this was an abundant valley, they lived as though starvation were imminent. Yet something inside told Buzz there was no need to worry; that they would naturally bee provided for, just like the ants and the caterpillars. Why couldn't they just slow their pace, have fewer mouths to feed, and let everyone relax and enjoy life a little more?

Buzz gazed up at the jagged peaks ringing the head of the valley. What was it like up there? And what was beyond? Rumor had it that the land beyond was inhospitable to bees. Some said it was covered with snow and glaciers as far as

the eye could see. Others said it dropped off precipitously to an arid desert. One thing was for sure — no one had ever tried to fly over. It was something bees just didn't do. Buzz himself had flown far enough up-valley to know that once you got above treeline you were at the mercy of the cold, harsh winds that always seemed to be blowing up there. Still, he couldn't help wondering.

A drone whizzed by: "Buzz, get your rear in gear." It seemed that every time he began to enjoy himself, someone came along and spoiled it. Buzz made for the meadow, loaded up again and returned to the hive. The responsible part of him knew he had to do his share, and he felt a bit guilty for his behavior today. He was, after all, a worker bee and workers are made to work — to build the hive, feed the larvae, keep house, forage, store honey and pollen, and defend the colony against attack. This latter task was particularly repugnant to Buzz. He hoped he would never be called upon to fight.

All afternoon Buzz forced himself to

do the task at hand and tried not to think about all the things that plagued his curious mind. He was, after all, only a bee, he reminded himself. He wasn't going to solve the problems of the world alone. He lived in an industrious society where it was very important to fit in. Already some of his friends were avoiding him, and he didn't want to bee a complete outcast. From now on, he would muster up some self-discipline and really apply himself. It would bee fine; after all, none of the other bees were complaining.

Buzz spent the next several days working as hard as he had ever worked in his life. No one could dare accuse him of beeing lazy now. Back and forth, back and forth he flew from hive to clover, always returning with a full load. He hoped that working would distract his mind. He had heard the elders say, "An idle mind is the devil's workshop," and he was beginning to believe it. All his thinking ever got him was trouble. He told himself that all he really wanted was to fit in.

At times Buzz was almost able to convince himself of this. He would make two or three round trips in a sort of automatic state, without thinking beyond the task at hand. Yet the truth of the matter was that, for the most part, he continued to think, to question, to bee curious. He just couldn't help it. Foraging was an instinctive activity that required little of his mind. Now he could both work and question it at the same time. It was starting to drive him crazy.

One morning before beginning the day's activities, several bees sitting on a branch close to the hive were observing ants swarming over the anthill below. Some were dragging a dead fly toward the nest, others were digging, but most just seemed to be scurrying about aimlessly.

"Look at those mindless ants," jeered one bee.

"Yeah, all they do is run around in circles all day," added another. "The only thing they care about is building a bigger nest and producing more ants. They don't know anything about how to appreciate life. It all seems so pointless."

Buzz could hardly believe his ears —

these were the same thoughts he had been having about their own colony! He couldn't contain himself: "But what makes the ants any different from us?"

"Different from us?" retorted the first bee. "Why everything. For one thing, we're a lot bigger."

"But size doesn't mean anything; it's all relative," responded Buzz.

"Maybe, but they all look alike; you can't tell one from another."

"Plus, *we* can fly," added the second bee.

"But still," protested Buzz, "we're both living creatures just experiencing life in our own ways."

"You miss the point, Buzz," a third bee added patiently. "Bees are simply a much higher form of life than ants. Look at the complexity of our hive, the intricacy of our social structure, the marvel of our reproductive capacities, the way we store honey. Ants can't even make honey; they can't begin to compare with us in these areas."

"But I'll bet ants also know a lot that we don't," Buzz shot back. "None of us has ever seen the inside of an ant nest. They seem to do a pretty good job of feeding and reproducing themselves. In fact, I'll bet their colony is larger than ours."

Buzz could see he was getting himself into hot water. Although a few of the bees flew off, most stayed, mumbling and exchanging glances of dismay, waiting for the leaders to settle this question once and for all. Finally, one authoritative voice spoke up.

"Quiet, quiet. QUIET! The real difference between us and them still hasn't been addressed. Each of those ants represents only a small piece of their colony; they have little sense of themselves beyond that. We are individuals, aware of ourselves and our surroundings. We have free will to do whatever we please."

Buzz saw red. "FREE WILL? How can you say we have free will when all we do, day after day, is build the nest, forage and tend the brood?"

"Because, young bee, we have the freedom to choose what part of the nest we work on, which flower to draw nectar from, the route we take to fly there and back, and which larvae to feed. What more freedom could a bee want?" By now a fairly large crowd was assembled, rumbling in agreement.

Buzz could see he was getting nowhere; he might as well be arguing with the sky. And whatever goodwill he had generated for himself these last few days was quickly beeing used up. It was hopeless. He shook his head and, without saying another word, lifted off and headed deep into the forest. There was general agreement among the gathered crowd that the truth had been successfully defended.

Buzz flew aimlessly through the woods, totally dejected. It had happened again. It wasn't intentional, but before he knew it he seemed to be making a fool of himself, isolating himself further from the rest of the colony. What was wrong with him? Why couldn't he fit in? He landed on the sand along the edge of a gurgling stream and stared blankly at the water swirling by.

"Don't let 'em get you down, young fella." Startled, Buzz looked up to see a rather haggard-looking, old bee with only one antenna landing next to him. "I saw what happened back there....felt like you could probably use a little encouragement."

"Thanks," mumbled Buzz half-heartedly.

"Name's Bert," offered the old-timer.

"I'm Buzz."

"I know. Everybody in the colony knows who you are by now."

Buzz winced. Bert continued. "I've been watching you. You're different; always have been and always will bee. I know it can bee difficult at times, but I consider beeing different an honor. It's God's way of trying to improve us, but it'll never happen if you stifle it."

Buzz was comforted by the knowledge that he wasn't the only bee in the colony to have such strange inclinations. Yet he didn't see much hope in Bert's advice. "But every time I open my mouth I seem to put my foot in it. If I speak my mind, I'm an outcast. If I stifle myself, I'm miserable."

"You've got to find middle ground, son," Bert responded. "Look, you're a worker and you've got to do your share if you're going to live in this colony. Yet that doesn't mean you can't bee who you really are. It's not work that's keeping you from beeing content; it's your attitude about work — thinking that work is separate from your personal life; that work is the sole point of life. You can work and think at the same time; I've seen you.

You can work and appreciate the beauty of this valley at the same time. And you can certainly mix a little relaxation and exploration into your daily routine. It's all a state of mind. Bee *in* the world; not *of* it."

"But what about all the other bees who are wasting their lives working, working, working, day after day 'till they drop dead?"

"Don't bee so concerned about them, Buzz. They're doing what feels right to them, just like you. And another thing — don't bee so worried about what they think of you. They've got different priorities, and if you spend your life trying to please them, you'll bee miserable. Just do your part and let your life, not your words, influence them."

Bert's kindly, soft-spoken manner impacted Buzz deeply, and he was already starting to feel better. Maybe there was hope after all.

Over the next several days Buzz tried to follow Bert's advice, but without much luck. The routine still made him numb. It seemed that the more he applied himself, the more he was drawn by the distractions of the valley.

"Just go with it and see what happens," suggested Bert one day when Buzz brought it up. "You're obviously beeing drawn to these other things for a reason. Why don't you find out what it is?" Still, Buzz felt guilty even considering the prospect of "goofing off."

That evening at sunset, he was preening himself following a particularly difficult afternoon. Flowers were very sticky places, and Buzz always had lots of pollen, dust and dirt to remove from his nectar-coated body.

Dusk was his favorite time of day; it always seemed to give him a greater sense of himself, of life. Everything was perfectly quiet — the air was still, the bees were all back at the hive, and the birds had stopped singing except for the occasional call of a distant whippoorwill.

The western sky was alive with color — first orange, then peach, then pink, and then finally a deep, dark blue. A thin mist had settled over the meadow and Buzz felt a hint of dew as the evening's first star came into view. He felt so peaceful; this was what it was really all about, he thought.

As dusk slowly faded into night, Buzz quietly sat there, lost in the timeless peace and beauty of the moonlit meadow. Finally the evening chill sent a shiver through his body, and he reluctantly lifted off back for the hive. He was careful to approach it discretely so as to avoid drawing attention to the fact that he had been out at night again. That was another thing bees just didn't do.

The next morning before heading off to the meadow, Buzz overheard a group of bees participating in their morning devotions. He had never thought much about religion, but this morning for some reason he felt drawn to the group. He positioned himself toward the rear and listened. The leader was just finishing a prayer: "....and finally, Lord, we ask that all those in the colony who have not yet accepted your word be shown the way so that they too may bee saved. Amen."

"Saved?" Buzz thought. "Maybe this is what I've been looking for." He mingled with the crowd, listening to the conversation, trying to get more information without drawing attention to himself. He overheard someone say, "....it just goes to show you, the love of honey is the root of all evil." Buzz thought this sounded a bit inconsistent, given that these were among the most honey-hungry bees in the colony.

The leader, Bobby, had his eye on Buzz ever since he had first slipped into the back of the group. He well understood what Buzz had been going through. He had seen it a thousand times and felt a sense of compassion for the confused young bee. Knowing the exact solution to Buzz's problems, he became excited at the prospect of making another convert. Bobby gradually made his way through the crowd toward Buzz and, when he was finally next to him, casually asked, "Aren't you the bee who's been asking so many questions lately? Well, we welcome you; you've come to the right place. I can imagine you've been a bit distraught and, you know, if you just turn your life over to the Lord, you too can bee saved."

"Saved from what?" Buzz asked.

"Why from hell; from eternal damnation when you die."

"But why would I go to hell?"

"Because you're a sinner, son, just like the rest of us. And if you don't live a pious life and ask God, the Supreme Beeing, for forgiveness, you don't stand a chance of going to heaven."

The notion that he was a sinner was news to Buzz. He had always considered himself to bee highly moral. Maybe he wasn't perfect, but he never did anything to maliciously hurt anyone. But then again, maybe the Supreme Beeing took a different view of things. These bees certainly seemed to know. Buzz wanted to hear more about the consequences of beeing a sinner. "What's hell like?" he asked.

Squinting his eyes, Bobby looked Buzz straight in the face and spoke in a foreboding voice. "Hell is like an eternal forest fire, with no escape and no relief, ever. Although the pain is unbearable, you never die; you just live in misery with all the other damned bees crying and moaning in agony forever."

Something didn't feel right, but Buzz wanted to hear more. "What's heaven like?"

A rapt expression overcame Bobby's face as he looked skyward. "Heaven is eternal paradise. It's an infinite, lush meadow filled with tasty wildflowers of every description. There's no need to work and there's never any discord. There are no bears and the weather's always perfect. All the bees' needs are provided for and everyone is happy all the time."

It actually sounded a bit boring to Buzz. "Can ants go to heaven?"

"No, only bees," responded Bobby authoritatively.

"But we don't go there till we die?"

"Right; if you're good and believe in the Supreme Beeing."

"But what about *this* life, the one we're living right now?"

"This life is simply preparation, a test for the hereafter."

It was all beginning to sound a bit contrived. If Buzz were going to believe all this, he wanted to see some benefits in this life, not on the chance that he'd be rewarded if there were a hereafter. "What's the Supreme Beeing like?"

"The Supreme Beeing is spirit which is everywhere and all-powerful. He is our creator who created us in his likeness, which means that he thinks and acts like a bee. This is how we know his wishes. He loves us and watches over us."

"But if he loves us, why would he send us to hell?" It was an honest question, but Buzz had just gone one step too far.

Bobby was having difficulty maintaining his smile. "You ask too many questions, young bee. This religion can't be figured out; you just have to accept it on faith."

Buzz didn't want to start another

argument and was about to take off when another bee who had been listening to the conversation spoke up. "I know this all must sound a bit confusing to you at first, son, but it starts to fit together after a while. It really all boils down to brotherly love."

Buzz couldn't believe his ears. This was the same bee he had heard cracking wasp jokes the day before! He had heard enough. As he lifted his wings to take off, Bobby invited him to devotions that night. Buzz thanked him, said he needed time to think it all over, and took off for the meadow.

Buzz was more confused than ever. All his life he had felt an intuitive knowing of God — a sort of oneness with nature — and that there was no need to formalize it. Yet now that he felt a greater yearning, what he was hearing just didn't fit at all. Although he tried to distract himself with work, it just made things worse. He finally broke away from his routine to find Bert.

"Religion doesn't come from God; it comes from bees," offered Bert. "Most folks don't know how to find God on their own, so they rely on others to show them the way. Problem is, God is within, and

"RELIGION DOESN'T COME FROM GOD; IT COMES FROM BEES"

most bees have a hard time believing they're divine. So they look outside themselves in religion or rituals to try to satisfy their longing for God."

Now this was making sense. Bert continued, "You're a different sort of bee, Buzz. The only place you're going to find the peace you're searching for is within. You can't go on looking to the rest of the colony for your well-beeing, because they don't have it to give to you."

As reluctant as he was to admit it, Buzz knew that Bert was right. "But

Bert," he protested, "it seems like the more I look within, the more miserable I become."

"I suggest you spend less time thinking and more time following your heart."

"How do I do that?"

"Well, the first step is to pay more attention to your feelings and those inner urges of yours. God's trying to tell you something and you're ignoring him. Honor your experience; that's how God speaks to you."

"What's the next step?"

"Following through; acting on it."

"But Bert, that means beeing so different and it feels so scary. I just don't know if I can. Isn't it possible to bee spiritual without beeing so different?"

"Absolutely; spirituality is expressing exactly who you really are, regardless of how that looks to others. Passion is the highest form of spirituality."

Buzz kicked loose a grain of pollen stuck to his leg and gazed out over the meadow, trying to absorb Bert's meaning. "Yeah, I guess I'm afraid I'll bee a failure."

"Who's to say what's failure and what's success; either way, you've grown. Ultimately, success is beeing on your path; gaining the experiences and lessons appropriate for your unique development. Only through experience can we expand beyond our limited bee perspective and start to see the larger picture of things."

"What's that?"

"You're probably asking the wrong bee, Buzz. I've only glimpsed it a few times, but I can tell you that once you've experienced it, you know once and for all that everything is perfect; that this universe is without flaw."

"Perfect? Without flaw?" Buzz felt his defenses coming on. "How can you say everything is perfect when there is so much prejudice and hostility and sickness and death in this valley? When I'm so unhappy lately? Are you saying all this is perfect?"

"From an expanded perspective, yes; they're all just opportunities for us to learn the lessons necessary to realize our own perfection. Let me ask you a question. Do you believe God is everywhere?"

"Well, yes, of course."

"Do you believe God is perfect?"

"Yes."

"Then, by definition, everything is perfect. Don't you see? Perfection isn't a state of affairs; it's a state of mind."

"Hmmm." At some level, Bert's words felt right to Buzz, but he was struggling to comprehend them intellectually. "You mean even unhappiness is perfect?"

"Yep, because it causes us to look deeper. Anytime I'm unhappy or angry or whatever, I try to see it as feedback that my consciousness is out of sync with God. To me, that's hell. It's not always easy and it takes discipline, but I believe the reason we're all here is to realize our oneness with God."

Buzz was getting angry again. This seemed like a heck of a lot of work and discipline, much more difficult than just doing his job as a worker bee, and he said so to Bert.

"It can bee that way at times, especially at first, but after a while the truth of it starts to sink in. It sure makes life a lot more satisfying in the long run."

"Satisfying? I want to bee happy and...."

"Never sad," Bert interrupted prophetically.

"Well, yes. What's wrong with that?"

"I suppose you also want up without down, soft without hard, and cold without hot?"

Buzz was caught off guard. His mind was reeling; he was speechless. Bert continued. "Don't you see, Buzz? Everything is relative; the instant you define one condition, you've created the other. How can you have cold unless you know what hot is? How can you have up without down? Happy without sad?"

Buzz gazed across the meadow, disappointment etched in his face. Bert was dropping yet another bombshell on him. "Are you telling me I'm going to bee unhappy the rest of my life?"

"No; only when you're unhappy. You can't avoid unhappiness, just like you can't seek happiness. Happiness can't bee pursued; it must ensue. It's a by-product of beeing who you really are. The minute happiness becomes a goal, you've set yourself up for disappointment."

"But Bert, you seem to bee happy most of the time."

"Buzz, most of what you see in me isn't happiness as much as it is peace; the inner peace that comes from accepting this valley just the way it is."

"SPLAT!" A large drop of rain hit the ground not a foot away. They looked up to see that the intensity of their conversation had distracted them from a thunderstorm building above. The sky had grown dark and a cool wind was kicking up. One of the cardinal rules of beeing was "Don't get caught in the rain;" a bee with waterlogged wings is totally useless. Buzz and Bert bolted for the nearest boulder, scrambled underneath and peered out intently as the storm grew.

Buzz flinched as lightning crashed into the top of a nearby tree. A gust of wind suddenly blasted through, whipping the tree tops like blades of grass. The sky was dark and ominous, but uncannily reluctant, yielding only sporadic, large raindrops. The storm seemed to bee toying with them. Buzz had never sensed such tension.

And then suddenly, it let loose. Driven by a roaring wind, curtains of rain raced horizontally across the meadow. Lightning crashed almost continuously, its thunder jolting the ground they stood on. It lit the meadow in bright eery flashes that sent chills down Buzz's spine. He glanced nervously at Bert in time to see the cold whiteness reflecting an excited smile on the old bee's face. Buzz tried to relax.

Gradually the wind and lightning subsided and the storm eased into a steady downpour. Water began trickling in to where they stood, forcing them to higher ground. Still the two bees stood there silently, each absorbed in his own thoughts. Buzz had always loved rain; it had a way of opening him up. The world always seemed a little different after a good thunderstorm. He thought back to what Bert had been saying about perfection.

"How do you know all this stuff you've been telling me?" he asked.

"I just pay attention. And I'm very careful about believing what I hear from other bees; I always check it out inside first." Bert stared blankly into the rain, giving Buzz the feeling his mind was somewhere far away. "Don't you see, it's perfect that we think that life is imperfect. It's what keeps each of us on our own unique path until eventually we all realize our own perfection, our oneness with God. In my book, that's heaven."

"But what's the point of it all?"

"The point is whatever it is for you. But when I look around I do see one factor common to all life, and that is expansion. Every bit of life seems to be trying to fill a greater niche."

The more Buzz heard, the more upset he was becoming. "But Bert, this whole expansion mentality is exactly what drives me crazy about this colony."

"I'm not just talking about *outer* expansion. There's plenty of that going on; too much, it seems at times. But then I'm not really one to say. I'm talking about that whole other world of *inner* expansion — what you're going through. It seems to me that both are appropriate; what's needed is more balance between the two."

Buzz nodded in thoughtful agreement. He noticed that the rain had just about stopped. "And we do that by looking within and seeking our true identity."

"Right; our basic problem is that we perceive ourselves as separate, apart from God. But God isn't some giant spirit bee in the sky. God is everywhere and everything — you, me, this boulder, the meadow, the sky....even Boris."

A quarter mile away Boris Bear was rambling through the woods when an ever-so-slight scent of honey wafted by his nose. It reminded him once again of the sweet treasure that was always so close, yet so far away. He had learned the hard way as a cub that, although bees are small, they can sure cause a bear a lot of pain. Through sheer determination he had managed to get a taste of honey then, and had never forgotten that it was by far the most delectable item on the forest menu. Boris decided to check out the hive, just on the remote chance that it had been deserted or something. When it came to honey, no stone was to be left unturned.

Buzz was storing a fresh load of pollen when he heard the alert go out. Heart pounding, he made his way through the frantic mob to the entrance of the hive and looked down. His worst fears were confirmed. Five feet below, Boris clung to the tree, trying to climb and swat bees off his face at the same time.

This was a life or death situation to the colony, or at least so Buzz had been told. All workers were to automatically attack the intruder without concern for the fact that those who stung him would die. Buzz had been rebuked when he once asked why they couldn't just rebuild the hive in a safer place and avoid all the loss of life. It was a matter of pride, he was told; they just couldn't let Boris push them around. Even though he was a clumsy oaf, he was big and they had to stand up to him. Buzz also sensed that some of the more macho bees actually wanted Boris to attack so they could taste

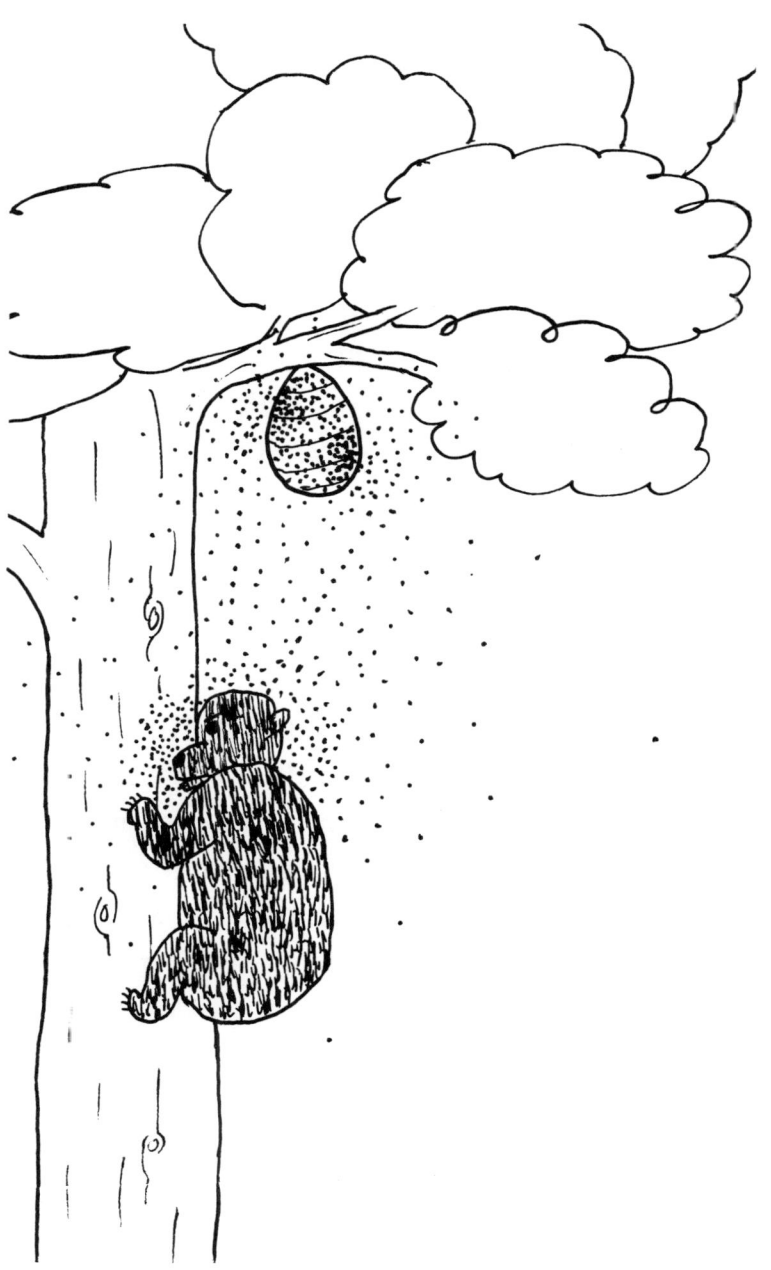

combat. He couldn't understand why they were so eager to die just for the sake of pride.

Buzz was pushed off the hive by the mass of bees taking to the air. Below, a swarm of them furiously orbited Boris's head. As soon as one bee stung him, it took off, mortally ripping its barbed stinger from its body, making room for another to attack. Buzz circled around the swarm, observing the carnage, but keeping his distance.

It was decision time for Boris. His face was a mass of bees; he couldn't even open his eyes for fear of getting stung in an eyeball. Growling and groaning, he finally realized that today wasn't his day for honey and began to retreat. Everyone breathed a sigh of relief except the macho bees, who pursued him all the way back into the forest.

The hive was a nightmare of wailing and moaning. Hundreds of mortally wounded bees returned with gaping holes in their rumps to die their slow deaths. Everyone was proud that the hive had been successfully defended, and this gave solace to the dying. Over the next two days a huge pile of dead bees accumulated beneath the hive. It was the most repugnant scene Buzz had ever witnessed, yet in some perverse way it seemed to build camaraderie among the colony. He couldn't understand it.

Just as things were returning to normal, a passing worker pointed at Buzz and said, "There's the coward." He couldn't believe it — he had been noticed! He tried to ignore it and move on, but one of the macho bees stepped in his path. "You sure kept your distance from Boris the other day."

Buzz felt his stinger throbbing, yet he remained calm. He remembered that Bert had cautioned him about not relying on others for his sense of well-beeing. Then he heard himself say, "I don't believe in war and I refuse to sacrifice my life for the pride of the colony. There are other ways to deal with Boris. If everyone felt the way I do, we wouldn't have that pitiful pile of dead bees down there."

"Boris is evil and must bee stopped. We can't just let him dictate to us how we live."

"But if we gradually move the hive to a safe place out of his reach, we'll never have to deal with him again," Buzz asserted.

"And what do you think that would do for the morale of the colony? We'd bee the laughing stock of the valley."

"Maybe for a while, but it would ultimately make us stronger because we wouldn't lose hundreds of workers every time Boris gets a craving for honey."

"Out of the question. Boris has to know he can't push us around."

Buzz's nerve was building and, on a hunch, he asked the macho bee a precarious question. "By the way, if you hate Boris so much, why are you here talking to me and not on that death heap down there?"

The other bee stuttered, "I...I...," but before he could finish, Buzz was gone.

Buzz couldn't stop thinking about what Bert had said about perfection. The old part of him wanted to dismiss it as total nonsense. How could 400 bees dying in a bear raid be perfect? Yet there was a new part of him that was excited by this notion; something rang true to the very core of his beeing.

One warm afternoon Buzz joined Bert basking in the sun on a dandelion puff. "Tell me how 400 bees dying in a bear raid is perfect."

"No, you tell me." Bert sensed that Buzz was getting lazy.

"Hmmmm. Well, I suppose first of all that there really is nothing evil about Boris liking honey. It just seems evil from our perspective because it happens to bee our honey he wants. Given all the pain we cause him, he probably thinks we're as evil as we think he is."

"Good. Say more."

"Well....although those bees dying seems to have been for the protection of the hive, it also has another purpose — to prod us to look for alternatives to enhance life. The denser we are, the harder the lessons. Those bees didn't have to die. The problem, though, is that most of the colony are either too lazy or proud or bound by tradition to seriously look for alternatives. But unless we do, we'll just keep making the same mistakes again and again. The perfection seems to lie in the process; in the opportunity for learning."

"Spoken like a true teacher!" Bert proudly stroked Buzz's antenna with his own. Buzz had never thought of himself as a teacher before.

"SPOKEN LIKE A TRUE TEACHER"

That far away look again spread over Bert's face. "Every incident that takes place here on the physical plane has its corollary on the spiritual plane — lessons. Lessons are the flip side of experience. Learning is what got us this far and is what will take us to wherever it is we're going. Although most bees see this world as an end unto itself, it's also a prop for learning, a vehicle for greater awareness."

Buzz felt a tingle spread through his body as this revelation dawned on him. "Bert, why didn't you tell me this before?"

"You weren't ready; wouldn't have understood."

Buzz couldn't argue with that. All this was so new; the bear raid really had driven the point home. "You know, you could say that those bees who died were my teachers, even though they didn't intend to be."

"Yep; we can all learn plenty from everyone — even those we think don't know as much as we do — if we can just set our egos aside. We're all each other's students and teachers."

Bert was getting warm and dropped into a shadow of one of the dandelion's leaves. Buzz just sat there thinking. "You know, this perspective stuff is amazing. Instead of viewing everything from inside out, it's like shifting your consciousness to perceiving things from outside in; moving out beyond our own bodies. It's like we can realize we're much more than bees. In fact if we expand far enough, it almost seems as though we can, in a way, become one with God."

Bert chuckled knowingly. "Does seem that way, doesn't it?"

As spring disappeared into summer, Buzz was spending more and more time with Bert who, it was becoming obvious, wasn't going to bee around much longer. The old-timer's body was finally giving in to the high-energy rigors of bee-ing. Although his mind was as sharp as ever, he had trouble staying aloft even a minute. And no one needed to say that once a bee can no longer fly, well....

Buzz found himself questioning everything. Occasionally he had glimpses of a new inner knowing, but more often than not felt a growing sense of pain and frustration. He'd have an hour or a day where he felt gloriously alive and one with the universe and happily think that he'd finally found what he was looking for. But sooner or later, usually sooner, he'd notice it fading away. Try as he might, there was nothing he could do to recapture it. Then, before he knew it, he was back in his old state of mind, which seemed even worse compared to what he had just experienced. It often hurt terribly — Buzz didn't know he could feel so bad, so unstable, so confused. It was times like these that he privately began questioning why he was spending so much time with Bert when all it did was upset him.

    Still, Buzz found himself intensely drawn to the pass. In fact, he could hardly stop thinking about it. One afternoon he flew up to treeline to take another look. It was definitely treacherous — the pass loomed another 1,500 feet above, the wind was whipping through the spruce trees and the thin air made for tough flying. The cold, grey rocks were a formidable contrast to the soft, green meadow. Yet something told him it was do-able.

Later that evening, Bert seemed to bee a little cold on the idea. "No matter where you go, there you are," he quipped.

"I suppose, but something tells me I need to find out what's on the other side."

"That's fine. Just don't think it's going to solve your problems." Buzz was reluctant to admit it, but he knew Bert was right. He was starting to get a little tired of Bert always beeing right. Bert continued, "Now, tell me about this urge of yours."

"Well, it's hard to describe. It's like I'm obsessed; I can't get it off my mind. It just seems like I've got to try it."

"Sounds like God's trying to tell you something. What's holding you back?"

"What's holding me back? It's dangerous up there! The wind blows like crazy and it's a long way straight up. I could get killed — that's what's holding me back."

"If you're afraid to die, you're afraid to live."

"Easy for *you* to say," Buzz shot back. Bert's triteness was really bugging him. Buzz could never quite figure him out. One minute he was against the idea and the next he was for it. "Bert, I know you're trying to help me, but sometimes I get so frustrated by all your doubletalk. Why don't you just come right out and tell me what you think I should do?"

Bert sensed the tension in Buzz's voice. "It pains me to see you struggling, Buzz, and sometimes I do want to give you advice, but what's right for me isn't necessarily right for you."

Buzz's frustration was mounting. "Sometimes I just wish I could go back and start over and bee just like everyone else," he pouted.

"There's no turning back now; you know too much."

"Great," Buzz grunted sarcastically.

A long, uncomfortable silence ensued. Buzz wished he had never been born, and said so to Bert.

Bert was sympathetic: "It doesn't all have to bee pain and effort you know.

Life's too important to bee taken seriously. Why don't you just give it to God?"

"How do I do that?" Buzz asked, only half interested.

"You need do nothing. Just bee. It's what you've been doing all along anyway, you just weren't aware of it. It's impossible to express anything other than God, but it's entirely possible to bee unaware of it."

Buzz looked up at Bert with a quizzical, hopeless expression. He obediently began trying to understand Bert's meaning, when a flash of rage exploded through him. "What is that supposed to mean?" he snapped. "Why can't you talk straight to me? Here you've screwed me up for life and you just keep feeding me more! And what's worse is I keep taking it! I'm sick and tired of you and all your mystical mumbo-jumbo! None of it makes sense; all it does is make me miserable! I'm getting out of here!"

Buzz was furious. He lifted off and headed for the solace of the forest, but quickly circled back around and whizzed by Bert, screaming at the top of his lungs, "LEAVE ME ALONE; I CAN'T TAKE ANYMORE!"

Buzz headed deep into the forest to his spot by the stream and fumed the rest of the day. Back and forth, back and forth he paced by the water's edge. Here his life seemed to bee falling apart, and his best friend was responsible. What right did that old loony have to brainwash him like this? Buzz secretly wished Bert would die soon, so he wouldn't have to see him again. It would sure solve a lot of his problems. Then he could get back to beeing normal again. He wondered how long it would take.

The next day, Buzz purposely avoided Bert. He decided that although the old-timer was well-meaning, he was getting senile and he just didn't need any more of his "wisdom" for a while. Buzz needed to concentrate his efforts on regaining his sanity.

At day's end he was heading back to the hive when, out of the corner of his eye, he saw a bee lying on the ground, obviously in trouble. Buzz dipped down to see if there was anything he could do, when he saw it was Bert, pathetically trying to stand. Immediately a wave of remorse and love melted his callousness as he saw his old friend struggling in vain. Bert was obviously dying.

Buzz landed quickly and tried to comfort him, tears streaming down his cheeks. "I'm sorry, Bert. I'm so sorry," he sobbed. "Please forgive me."

"Nothing to bee sorry about, son," Bert whispered, obviously in pain. "You did what you had to do." Bert smiled at Buzz in a way that said, "All is forgiven."

Buzz propped the old bee's head up as best he could, overwhelmed with love for him. "Thank you so much for all you've given me, Bert. I'll always remember you."

Bert just winked. "Pass it on."

Buzz was surprised at the peace in Bert's face. "You haven't said a word about dying. Aren't you afraid?"

"Only when I forget who I really am,"

he whispered. "I've learned all I can in this body and now I'm ready to take the next step."

Bert looked so peaceful it was hard to believe he was dying. He grimaced, took a few deep breaths and then continued haltingly. "Listen to me Buzz. You've got a rare gift for finding the truth. But finding it is only half the game. The other half is that you have to live it. Do you understand me, son? The truth doesn't mean anything unless it's manifest in life. Don't just tell the truth; *live* it!"

Bert's breathing grew shallow, and Buzz comforted him as best he could. He wanted to say something but was having a hard time finding the breath to do it. Finally he pulled Buzz close and whispered faintly, "...early...morning."

Bert died with a smile on his face.

Buzz passed most of the night in tears. Bert was the only bee he had ever loved, the only bee who ever understood him, and now he was gone. Buzz already missed him terribly. He didn't know he could feel so alone, so sorrowful. It was the longest, saddest night of his life.

Buzz sobbed and sobbed until there were just no more tears left. Still he stood there, silently mourning his old friend into the wee hours of the new day. Eventually a feeling of restlessness began to overcome him. What was he going to do now? He had to leave Bert sooner or later. Once, he left to return to the hive, but it just didn't feel right so he flew back to continue his vigil, staring sorrowfully into the lifeless but peaceful face of the old bee. He knew that it had been more than luck that Bert had appeared in his life when he did. The old-timer had given him so much, but now what was he supposed to do with it?

His mind was exploding with all that had been said, but it kept coming back to one thing: "Live the truth." He knew that the truth for him was to find out what was on the other side of those mountains. He could think about it and talk about it to the day he died, but until he did it, he would be living a lie.

Buzz made his final peace with Bert and was off at the first hint of dawn. It was difficult flying in the cold greyness, but he couldn't wait any longer. As he arrived at treeline, alpenglow lit the peaks in a pinkish orange. Buzz gazed up in awe. This truly was a miraculous place and, from now on, he was going to experience more of it.

He fed on a few wildflowers to build

his energy and then surveyed the range. It was still intimidating. But something else was bothering him; something didn't feel right. He tried to discern what it was, but with no luck. He was getting nervous, having second thoughts. "What am I doing up here?" he asked himself. "I must bee crazy. That wind is going to obliterate me on those rocks."

And then it hit him. "WIND? THERE IS NO WIND!" he screamed inside. It was as though the air, in its silence, was beckoning him: "Come on; you can do it!" His body shuddered with excitement as the adrenalin rush boosted him upward. As the valley floor receded below, Bert's words seemed to reverberate off the mountain:

Passion is the highest form of spirituality.

"Bert!" Buzz thought. "So this was what he was trying to tell me when he said 'early morning.' Has he been up here?"

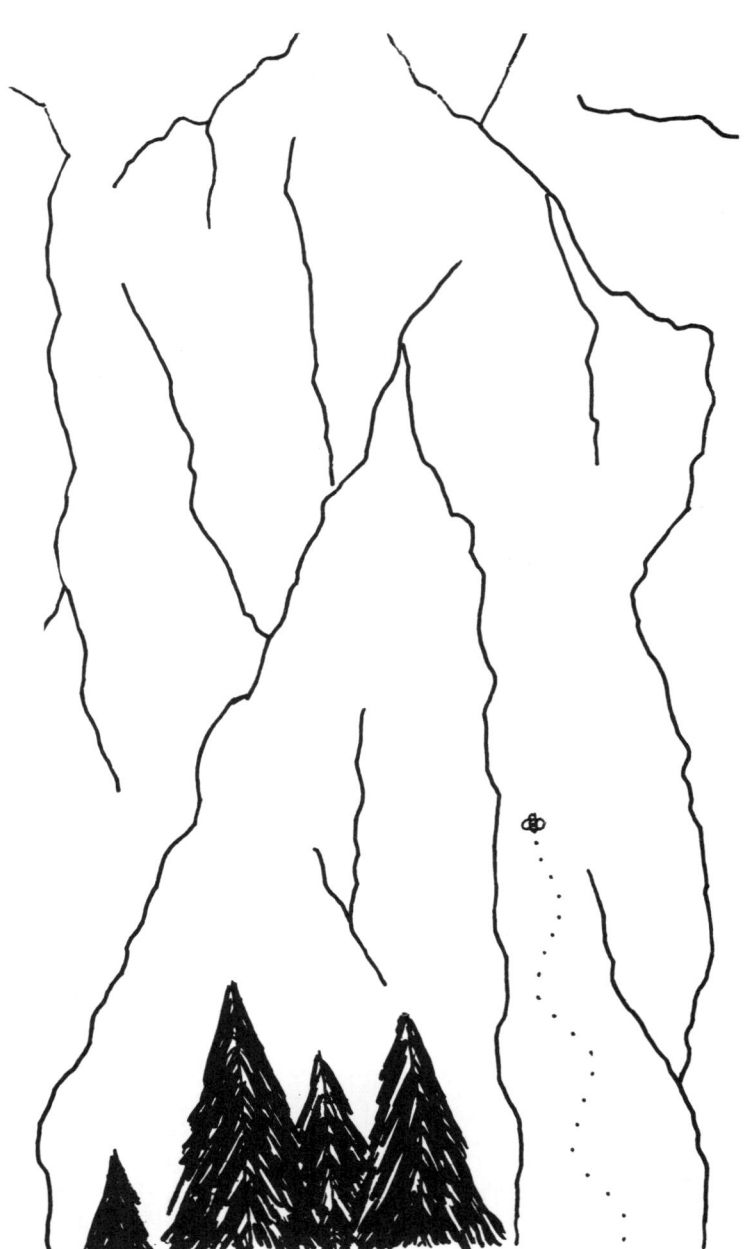

The first 500 feet went by like a jaunt to the meadow, before the realities of bee physiology caught up with Buzz. He hovered for a moment, regaining his energy, and surveyed the scene below. One thing was for sure — he had never been this high before. Down-valley the meadow looked like a tiny green patch on the valley floor. Above, another 1,000 feet of sheer rock face seemed to mock his brazen intent. He continued climbing, this time at a more reasonable pace.

As he approached the halfway point, Buzz began feeling drained. His tiny wings had never been called on to do this kind of duty. He landed on a small rock outcropping to rest, and as he sat there, this tiny bee overseeing his magnificent valley, the reality of what he was doing finally hit him.

It was pristinely beautiful. The air was perfectly pure and crisp. To the left, a thin waterfall misted to the valley floor. A hundred shades of green were absorbing the brilliant sunshine. Beaver were out for their morning swim. Deer were grazing. Clouds drifted by, closer than ever before. Distant birdsong filled the air. Everything seemed alive!

"It truly is all perfect," Buzz said slowly to himself. "It all fits together; everything complements everything else. There are no mistakes. Good and bad **are** only within the minds of bees. It all just IS!" His body tingled with the impact of his profound realization; he was ecstatic.

*Happiness cannot bee pursued;
It must ensue.*

So this was what Bert meant when he talked about happiness cropping up out of nowhere when you're beeing who you really are. A gust of wind brought Buzz back to the moment. If he were going to fly this pass today, he needed to get going because a breeze was already kicking up. He lifted off and continued to climb — another 200, 300, 400 feet. Yet the higher he got, the more the breeze became wind, and the tougher it was to maintain control.

He felt himself beeing buffeted about and missed smashing into a rock outcropping by a mere two feet. A downdraft erased 100 feet of vertical progress in four seconds. Buzz sensed disaster and fought desperately to pull away from the rocks. His tiny wings were beating with everything he had, but he was running out of energy. He needed to land, and soon, but the air was far too unstable to approach the rocks. Buzz Bee was in big trouble and he knew it.

Then came the gust he had been dreading. The last thing he remembered was frantically reversing as he was thrust at the side of the mountain, totally out of control.

Buzz's first impression when he came to was surprise that he was alive. He looked around in disbelief. The wind had tossed him onto a narrow shelf 300 feet below the summit. He was groggy and weak and depleted, but he was alive. As he regained his senses, he slowly realized there was no way he could go any higher in this condition; in fact, there was no way he could go anywhere in this condition. He needed nectar, and badly.

He crawled back and forth, surveying his situation for any possibility of escape. Up, down, right, left — the only options were sheer rock face and roaring wind. Flying was out of the question. Slowly

Buzz came to the realization that it was all over.

He felt numb. His ears began ringing. He couldn't believe it — he, Buzz Bee, was going to die. Not somebody else; he himself. Tomorrow he just wouldn't bee here anymore. He was so young. How could this bee happening to him? Here he was following his dream and now he was going to die for it. So much for living your truth. The world truly was an unfair place! A thousand thoughts raced uncontrolled through his terrified mind.

He tried to think of dying as going to sleep and just not waking up, but somehow it didn't seem to comfort him much. He wondered what it would bee like to starve to death, and how long it would take. He imagined what would happen to his body — it would dry out, a gust of wind would blow it off the edge and it would bounce all the way down the rocks to the bottom. Then it would just lie there and rot. And no one would ever even know, or care, for that matter. It was all so terribly sad. Buzz cried, he quivered, he screamed and he wailed but his fear only grew worse.

He sat there for the rest of the morning, agonizing over the inevitable. At times he was overcome by fear and sadness. But then he'd think that he didn't want to die that way and manage to get a hold of himself. For a while he'd bee able to rationally contemplate his life and death. But then his mind would get away from him and the fear and sadness would overwhelm him all over again.

Gradually Buzz felt himself becoming groggy. He could hardly move and was having a difficult time thinking clearly. Everything was becoming fuzzy and dreamy. It was a pleasant respite from his earlier terror, and Buzz welcomed it. It really wasn't such a bad way to go after all.

He was fading in and out of consciousness when, out of nowhere, he tasted honey in his mouth. He sat up with a start. How could he bee tasting honey? He hadn't had any since dawn and his body was totally depleted. He dismissed it as a hallucination and began to lie back down.

Then suddenly, out of the corner of his eye, he saw them. At first he thought he was dreaming; he looked away, rubbed his eyes and then looked back again. They were still there — a small clump of three, tiny, purple wildflowers miraculously clinging to the cold, lifeless granite. He still couldn't quite believe it. What was going on? He had spent the entire morning on this shelf. How could he possibly have overlooked them? Was he dreaming?

Buzz dragged his depleted little body over to the flowers and touched one. It was real! With all his might, he slowly climbed up, peered inside and saw, deep within, the tiny pistil, glowing with a thin coating of nectar. He squeezed inside and feasted. Nectar had never tasted so good! When he finished with the first flower, he moved on to the second, his energy slowly returning. By the time he was half done with it, Buzz was full and beginning to feel like his old self again.

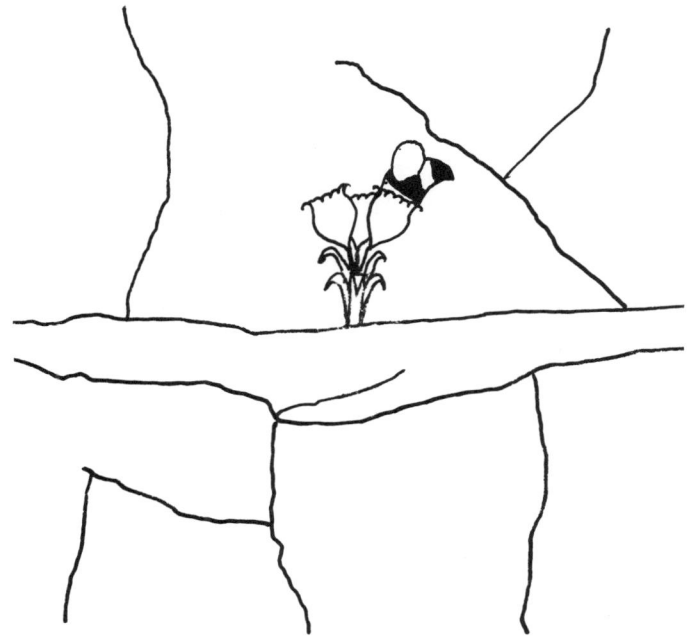

Suddenly the realization that he was going to live hit him. He was ecstatic! He wasn't going to die after all; he was going to live! Buzz was so relieved, so happy, so elated! All his senses were heightened — it felt so good to bee alive! He vowed never to take his life for granted again.

He looked back at the flowers, still not quite believing what had just happened. "What incredible luck," he thought to himself. "How did those flowers get there? In fact, why wasn't I killed in the first place when the wind slammed me against the rocks?" Exactly what *was* going on here this morning?"

Soon Buzz was beginning to feel like his old self again. He walked to the edge and looked down. A gust of wind blasted through, nearly blowing him off the edge. Buzz crouched, grasping a nub of granite until it passed. The wind was howling worse than ever and he knew there was no way he could take off until it died down. He found himself a sunny spot protected from the gale and relaxed. He knew that the wind usually died around sunset, and that at worst he'd probably just have to wait out the afternoon.

And so he sat, this bold little bee overlooking his homeland, feeling like a king. Buzz felt more alive than he had ever felt in his entire life; even more than when he was a youngster. He hummed his favorite bee tunes, a big smile plastered across his face, to pass the time. He knew now that he'd not only survive this ordeal, but that he was going to make it to the other side. Every once in a while he'd wander over to the flowers for a sip of nectar, and bee amazed all over again at his good fortune. God was smiling through Buzz Bee as he sang a tune to Bert's words:

Life is too important to bee taken seriously.

The sun dropped lower and lower in the sky and the wind continued to howl. Still, Buzz remained confident that it would die once the sun set. But when the sun touched the horizon and then slowly sank out of sight without a hint of change in the wind, Buzz began to worry. He knew he had only an hour of light and warmth left to make it over the pass. The wind screamed worse than ever, and when the first star came out, Buzz's spirits again sank.

He was going to have to spend the night up here, exposed to this freezing wind and he didn't know if he could make it. As the hours passed and the evening chilled, Buzz got colder and colder. He wedged himself into the most protected crevice he could find. Although the granite was dead cold, it was better than the wind. But soon he began shivering uncontrollably. He stepped back out onto the ledge to flap his wings and hop around, but it barely helped.

Buzz thought of his colony below, all protected and warm in the hive. It really wasn't so bad there after all. Why did he ever come up here? He realized how much he had there and what a fool he had been to take it all for granted. He began to think that if the wind died tomorrow, he would return and make a new life for himself. Just then the strongest gust of the night wailed through, seeming to shout Bert's words:

*There's no turning back now;
you know too much.*

Twice, in the wee hours of the morning, Buzz caught himself nodding off. It was the one thing he knew he couldn't let himself do, for if he didn't keep moving, he knew he'd never wake up. He forced himself back out onto the shelf and hopped around. His feet were frozen, his body quaked and his wings ached, but he forced himself to move. It was pure agony.

And so Buzz Bee spent the longest, most miserable night of his life, alternating between crevice and shelf; trying to keep warm, trying to stay alive.

Finally, after what seemed like an eternity, Buzz noticed a faint greyness in the eastern sky and a lone bird singing in the distance. Bird singing? An hour before, he couldn't have heard a bird singing if it had been right next to him. He realized the wind had stopped; everything was perfectly still.

Dawn seemed to drag on forever. Buzz impatiently shivered through it, his anticipation the only thing keeping him alive. Finally sunlight struck the top of the pass and ever so slowly crept down the mountain. Buzz stiffly crawled to the highest point on his shelf and waited, quaking with cold. As the first rays of light hit him, tingles of pleasure surged through his body. Buzz never realized sunlight could feel so good; that was another thing he'd never again take for granted.

Gradually his frozen little body thawed and he began to feel like his old self. Buzz basked as never before, walking back and forth on the shelf, spreading his wings to the sun so as to catch every last ray of that wonderful warmth.

After taking a final sip of nectar, he was ready. He lifted off, and in the calmness of the morning air, was up and over the top of the pass in no time. It struck him how simple life was when he worked with nature, when he respected the truth, and how difficult it was when he worked against it.

The descent to the valley seemed to take forever. Once Buzz did a 180 and hovered there, staring up at those peaks, absorbing the significance of what he had just done. What an accomplishment! Buzz felt so proud. Not many other bees

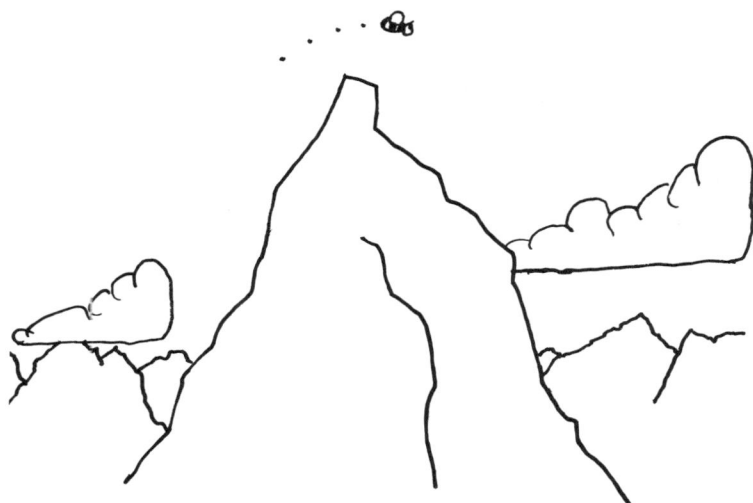

could have done what he just did.

The land below looked so beautiful and inviting. As he reached the valley floor, Buzz dipped into some clover to replenish his energy. He snickered to himself at the thought of the bees in his colony believing this side was a desert or covered with glaciers.

He could tell right away that things over here were different. The meadow was huge — it seemed to stretch forever, broken only by occasional clumps of trees and bushes. As far as he could see in every direction, there were bees, bees and more bees, busily engaged in morning foraging. The air felt electric. Already he could spot three hives scattered in trees here and there.

His first inclination was to explore, but as he lifted his wings to take off, Buzz realized how weak and tired he was; his ordeal was finally catching up with him. He gave a big yawn, found a nice shady spot to rest and immediately nodded off.

It was early afternoon before Buzz awoke. He lay there for a while, sleepily observing the bees on this side. Compared with those in his colony, they were relatively small, and seemed to have a relaxed, peaceful manner that Buzz found very appealing. He felt a bit conspicuous lying there, yet although several bees flew by and glanced at him, none seemed to pay him any particular notice. "This sure is different from my colony," he thought.

Finally he could no longer resist the urge to explore and took off. Life over here looked pretty much the same as the other side — the flowers, the trees, the birds, the deer. But at the same time, it felt different; somehow more comfortable. Buzz couldn't quite put his antenna on it.

As he flew by a hive, he was amazed at its enormity. Buzz guessed it was at least twice as large as his hive. How could these bees have such a huge colony with such a relaxed attitude?

He landed on a small granite boulder to decide what to do next. One thing was certain — he had to find a hive before sunset. He wasn't going to spend another night out in the cold. But nothing else seemed clear. He sat and sat, without one good idea coming along, and began to feel disappointed. Here he was in a strange land, didn't know a soul and now had no idea of what he was going to do. "Why did I come over here?" he asked himself. "What did I expect?" He realized he had never given any thought to what he might find over here. He just did it because of his crazy urge.

*No matter where you go,
there you are.*

Buzz spent the rest of the afternoon on that boulder, realizing the truth of Bert's words. He felt like such a stranger here. He was afraid to approach a hive and ask to stay with them, for fear of beeing rejected. What was he going to do?

Just then, another bee landed next to him, smiled and bowed. Buzz bowed back. The other bee just stood there looking curiously at Buzz, making him a bit uncomfortable. Buzz finally broke the silence: "Hi, I'm Buzz."

The other bee simply smiled and replied in a strange accent, "I know. Beebee's expecting you."

Buzz was surprised, to say the least. "Beebee? Who's Beebee? And how did she know I was coming?" .

The other bee giggled quietly and said, "Beebee knows everything. Come." And with that, the bee took off. Sensing that he was about to find out why he had flown over here, Buzz followed close behind.

They flew to a hive only a short distance away, and entered. Inside was the

"BEEBEE'S EXPECTING YOU"

most complex labyrinth of bee construction Buzz had ever seen. The sweet scent of honey was overwhelming. Buzz followed the other bee through several different passages deep within the hive and finally rounded a corner which opened to a fairly large chamber. There, in the middle, surrounded by a few drones, sat Beebee. She smiled at Buzz and beckoned him to come closer.

Buzz immediately noticed a warm,

peaceful feeling come over him. He had the overwhelming sense that everything was OK and somehow intuitively knew he was in the presence of a very special bee. Beebee was larger than the other bees, which made her about Buzz's own size. Although she was absolutely beautiful, it was her loving demeanor which affected Buzz the most. She smiled warmly at him and asked, "How are you?"

Buzz could barely talk. "I'm, uh, fine....now."

Beebee giggled. "You're welcome to stay here. Bees aren't meant to spend the night on mountains, you know. Do you have any questions?"

"DO YOU HAVE ANY QUESTIONS?"

This caught Buzz off guard. His mind was spinning with questions, but he didn't know where to begin. Finally he asked, "How did you know I was coming?"

Beebee giggled again and simply said, "Stay a while." With that she stood up, stretched her wings and announced, "Time to fly." She moved toward the entrance of the chamber and, as she passed by, Buzz tasted honey in his mouth. There it was again! He was dumbfounded; what was going on here?

By the time Buzz regained his senses, Beebee had disappeared into the passageway. He hurried after her.

By the time Buzz found his way back to the entrance of the hive, Beebee was quite a way off, accompanied by several drones. He took off and made a beeline for her. Already many workers had joined her, while those on the ground smiled and bowed as she flew over. Buzz got the sense that this was a regular occurrence with this colony.

After leisurely circling the meadow, Beebee landed. Within a few minutes, several hundred bees surrounded her. Buzz edged his way closer to the center of the crowd to see what was happening. Beebee stood there, all eyes glued to her, as several bees bowed at her feet asking for her help or blessing. She spoke with them briefly one at a time, and as she finished with each, some seemed consoled, while others remained distraught. It seemed like everyone wanted something from her and she patiently did what she deemed appropriate for each.

Suddenly excitement arose from the rear as several bees pushed their way through the crowd, carrying an old worker with a crippled wing, obviously near death. He gazed expectantly at Beebee, hoping she could help him. "My wing....it's worse. I'm getting weak and I can't fly anymore."

Beebee looked at him compassionately, sensing the love in the old bee's face. "Would you like to fly again?" she asked quietly.

"Oh yes! More than anything."

"Then fly."

Buzz again tasted honey. The worker stood up with an astounded look on his face and cautiously tested his crippled wing. He glanced confidently at Beebee, and then lifted off, hovering above the multitudes. The crowd gasped, and then lapsed into general chaos. Buzz picked out the words "messiah" and "savior" from the clamor. The worker landed and fell at Beebee's feet crying hysterically. "Thank you, thank you," he cried. "How can I ever thank you?"

Beebee replied simply, "Express God through your life." With that, she headed back for the hive, shining her serene smile over the crowd as she lifted off.

The rest of the bees chattered excitedly among themselves, while Buzz remained dumbstruck. He simply did not know what to make of all this; things were happening too fast. He headed into the woods to sort it all out.

Buzz landed on an aspen twig and began mulling it over. On the one hand, things were more confusing than ever. Exactly who and what was Beebee? What made her so loving and peaceful? How did she know he was coming? Where did that taste of honey come from? And how did she heal that worker? How?

But on the other hand, somehow it all seemed to fit. Buzz had always sensed there was more to life than it seemed on the other side, and now here was living proof. There was only one thing Buzz was sure of — whatever it was that was happening over here, he wanted more of it.

He sensed forces at work in Beebee that he had no knowledge of. And he intuitively knew he would never bee able to figure them out; they were simply beyond his comprehension. Try as it might, his mind just kept on short-circuiting. The one thing that stood out was

Beebee's love. She just seemed to bee pure love — evidently that was the source of her power. It didn't make sense, but that's what he felt. Maybe that was the key....

Needless to say, Buzz accepted Beebee's invitation to stay in their hive. The next morning he flew to the meadow with the other bees and began foraging. If he were going to live here, he needed to do his share. Rather than think about all that had happened, he tried to concentrate on the feeling he had beeing around Beebee.

It wasn't long before he struck up a conversation with another bee. Just like the others he had met, this bee was so sweet and unassuming. The first thing Buzz asked was, "Who is Beebee?"

"Beebee is God incarnate," replied the bee simply.

Buzz's mind immediately kicked in: "You mean God, the creator of the universe?"

"Yes."

"But God is everything, not an individual bee; don't you think?"

"God is also love, and Beebee is love. Look at the way she heals. And haven't you tasted honey when you're in her presence? She must bee God."

Buzz couldn't argue with that, but still something wasn't right. He had a hard time thinking of God as an individual bee, even if she did have mystical powers. Still, he envied the devoted, simplistic way the bee revered Beebee. Maybe that was what he needed to do.

Just then Buzz got an idea. If Beebee could make others taste honey, why couldn't he? He'd never tried; maybe it was possible. He looked at the other bee and concentrated with everything he had on making honey appear in his mouth.

The other bee was confused by the strained expression on Buzz's face, but thought perhaps it was just some strange mannerism of this foreigner. Finally he grew curious and asked Buzz if he was feeling well.

"Yes, yes," responded Buzz sheepishly. He realized he still had a long way to go.

Just then, both bees noticed a small swarm approaching them, led by Beebee. To Buzz's surprise, she began descending and landed next to him. Immediately she was surrounded by the rest of the swarm. Buzz again felt a sense of awe and wonder at her presence.

Beebee was radiant. "Are you feeling at home?" she asked.

Buzz felt a bit self-conscious beeing the center of attention, but managed a "Yes, thank you" in reply. Suddenly he noticed that he was the only bee not bowing down to Beebee and immediately dropped to his knees.

"Why do you do that?" Beebee asked.

"Because everyone else is doing it," Buzz replied, his forehead touching the ground.

"Oh," Beebee giggled. "How can I help you?"

The other bees looked enviously at Buzz. He wasn't going to let this opportunity slip by. "Are you really God?"

"Yes," replied Beebee. "And so are you. The only difference between us is that I know it and you don't."

"You mean if I were aware of my divinity, I'd bee like you?"

"No, you'd bee like you," she responded sweetly.

Buzz felt that familiar sense of confusion he used to have around Bert.

Beebee continued, speaking louder so everyone could hear, "God is like the ocean and we're all like drops in that ocean. Individually, we each contain all that is in the ocean — water, salt, the elements; we're all little God-parts. Combined we form God."

Buzz still wasn't satisfied. "Are you a messiah?"

Beebee responded with a question of her own. "What is a messiah?"

This caught Buzz off guard. He thought for a moment and then responded, "Isn't a messiah someone sent from God to save us?"

"To save you from what?" Beebee asked.

Buzz was getting frustrated. He wanted answers, not questions. "To save us from.....from all our pain and misery," he replied.

"As God, only you can do that. I can only bee an example. There are no messiahs or saviors; only masters and teachers."

Buzz had no trouble settling in to the routine on this side. Seeing Beebee everyday made it all worthwhile, even if it were only a glimpse as she flew over. She was everyone's source of hope and joy. A glance, a few words, a taste of honey — all were highly-prized acknowledgements that could send a bee into ecstacy. Beebee was the topic of almost every conversation, and Buzz just couldn't hear enough about her.

As the days passed, Buzz felt himself moving into a state of beeing he had never before experienced. He noticed he just didn't care as much about the things that used to concern him, and that his mind was slowing down. He had never felt so at ease, and found himself letting go of the need to control his life. Everything just seemed to take care of itself. He dwelled on Beebee most of the time, wondering about her and basking in her love. With her around, there was nothing to worry about.

By all outward appearances, the routine on this side was really not very different from that on the other side. Buzz still spent most of his days foraging and working. Only now his attention was mostly focused on God and Beebee, instead of resentment about having to work all the time. He was amazed at how pleasant and peaceful life could bee. Bert was right — it wasn't work; it was his attitude.

Bee in the world; not of it.

Buzz made many new friends over here, absorbing the love they radiated and reflecting it back to them. He no longer felt like a loner. Although his friends expressed little interest about Buzz's land, he couldn't hear enough about theirs. As time passed, he felt like he was becoming one of them. It was a pleasant respite from all the intensity earlier this summer.

Buzz also found that his concept of time was changing. He rarely noticed how many trips he made to the meadow or if he was getting enough done. He simply did what he did, moment by moment, and the days took care of themsleves. Eventually they all seemed to melt together, and one morning Buzz was surprised to feel a chill in the air. He couldn't believe fall was just around the corner. Where had the summer gone?

Buzz Bee had finally found what he was looking for. He was beginning to feel he could spend the rest of his life here. It was all perfect.

Well, almost. Actually there was one little thing that bothered him. It wasn't that important, but try as he might, he couldn't completely get it out of his mind. Every once in a while it just seemed to pop up out of nowhere.

It was Beebee's continuous talk that all bees are God. She said it equally to everyone in as many different ways as possible, but few seemed to really hear her. It was clear from their talk that they didn't think of themselves as divine, or even want to. They were content worshipping Beebee and didn't seem to have any intention of realizing their own Godhood.

Buzz felt that, if Beebee were really serious about what she said, she should be a little harsher with them to awaken them from their complacency. But all she did was smile and love, which just seemed to increase their dependency on her. It seemed so inconsistent; why did she do it? Did she secretly like beeing the center of attention and having all these admirers?

Whenever these thoughts came, Buzz would feel guilty. Who was he to second guess her? She was certainly far more advanced than he. Certainly she knew what she was doing. And then there was the fact that she was selflessly devoting her life to the colony. Still, something didn't feel right. Buzz's truth was again tugging at him.

One morning Buzz saw the familiar swarm flying in the distance and lifted off to join them. By the time he landed, Beebee was already surrounded by several hundred bees, talking quietly with a few in the center. Buzz always had questions for her and was often fortunate enough to catch her attention. Beebee finished with the bee she was talking to and scanned the crowd, face by face. The expectant look on Buzz's face betrayed his curiosity and Beebee laughed.

"Yes, Buzz?" She knew she could always expect a question from him.

"Beebee, why is it that you heal some bees and not others?"

Beebee addressed the entire gathering. "I alone have not healed anyone.

They have been healed by the divine part of themselves they experience through my presence. I'm not here to heal everyone or solve your problems. I'm here to show you how to solve your own problems, but it is in a way other than you expect. Bee open to what I say. No one can save you but yourselves."

"NO ONE CAN SAVE YOU BUT YOURSELVES."

There it was again. Buzz could resist no longer. "Then what are we all doing following you?" Several bees gasped, feeling Buzz was beeing disrespectful.

Beebee sensed his sincerity, though, and replied sweetly, "Why do you ask *me*?"

"I...I..." Buzz was speechless. Why *was* he asking her? Who would know the answer to that question better than he, himself?

From that day on, things were never quite the same. Try as he might, Buzz could never recapture that nice, peaceful feeling he had earlier. And Beebee wasn't helping matters any.

In fact, she only made it worse. Whenever he was in her presence, Beebee seemed to purposely ignore Buzz, passing over his face as she scanned the crowd. And Buzz never got those mystical tastes of honey any more, either, despite the fact that others were still getting them regularly. Why was she doing this? Was she angry with him? She hadn't seemed offended, despite his bold question. He decided it must have been something else.

Buzz searched for every possible reason for Beebee's disdain, thinking back over every encounter, trying to determine where he had erred. She had always been so open to him. Why was she ignoring him now? What had he done? If only he knew, he could make amends. He found himself becoming more depressed with each passing day.

Although he fought it, Buzz finally felt himself getting angry with Beebee. What gave her the right to treat him like this after the way he loved her? Many of the other bees who Buzz secretly thought were far less knowledgeable and spiritual than he seemed to capture her attention at will. As far as Buzz was concerned, this fickle side of her was exposing her for what she really was. Maybe he had been wrong about her, thinking she was perfect and all.

And so what if Beebee was clairvoyant and had healing powers? Exactly what did that mean? Was that reason enough for Buzz to surrender his life to her? She was still a bee, just a highly evolved one. Buzz felt that familiar old restless feeling growing inside. "Not again," he secretly bemoaned.

*Honor your experience;
   that's how God speaks to you.*

It had been wonderful beeing with Beebee, but Buzz began to realize maybe he didn't need to bee with her forever. Maybe it was time to move on. But what would he do next? Where would he go? He had become so comfortable over here. How could he possibly leave? The thought frightened him.

That night Buzz had a dream that wouldn't let him go. He was back at his old colony. Everything was white and everyone was frantically circling around a big blob on the ground. Buzz felt the need to help, but when he tried, no one saw him; he was invisible. They couldn't hear him either. He tried and tried to make himself seen and heard, but it was no use. Frustrated, he tossed and turned the whole night. When he finally awoke at the crack of dawn, Buzz knew it was time to return home.

Don't just tell the truth; live it!

As he made his way to the entrance of the hive, he passed Beebee's chamber and peeked in. She lay sleeping, as beautiful and serene as ever. Buzz felt a twinge of sadness that he would never bee able to say goodbye to her, but just as he turned to leave, he got that familiar, sweet taste of honey. In a flash, he understood everything. Beebee hadn't been mad at him. She was simply trying to awaken him from his complacency, to spur him to bee himself. That Beebee; she was really something!

The flight back over the pass was deceptively easy. Buzz didn't know if it was him or the quiet air, but he could hardly believe these were the same mountains which had given him so much trouble earlier. He took a short rest half way up and before he knew it, he was approaching the top. The dawn air was so still he decided to stop right on the summit to rest.

From this point he could see both valleys, and felt a special affection for each. Both had taught him so much, but somehow his homeland seemed to be calling him back now. He lingered there for a few minutes and then began the long descent home.

As he approached his old meadow, Buzz felt a wave of nostalgia come over him. There was the hive, busy as ever. These really were good bees, when you stopped to think about it. There was the aspen twig he used to daydream on, the rock he and Bert used to share. This truly was a good place to live. Buzz moved to his old twig and passed the morning reminiscing and getting the feel for this side again.

He wasn't quite sure how to approach the colony. After such a long time, they probably thought he was dead.

What was he going to tell them about where he'd been? About Beebee? They'd surely think he was crazy.

As mid-day approached, Buzz's attention was increasingly drawn to a huge black thunderhead building directly above. Suddenly a bolt of lightning sliced into a nearby ridge and a cold wind smelling of rain gusted up from nowhere. Just as Buzz decided to get to the hive — THUD! A huge ball of hail hit the ground, nearly grazing Buzz's wing! He instinctively dropped to the nearest boulder and scrambled underneath. Buzz's heart felt like it was about to pound right out of his chest; that was far too close for comfort! Few bees ever lived to tell about encounters with hailstones. Rain was one thing; hail was quite another.

THUD!......THUD!..THUD!THUD! In no time the whole meadow was transformed into a scene of bouncing hailstones two and three times the size of bees. Buzz saw several bees who lingered too long blasted right out of the air by the deadly flashes of ice. Many others miraculously made it to the hive, only to find no place to land due to the sudden mass retreat. As they circled waiting for landing space, the hail intensified, pounding them mercilessly to the ground. Buzz yelled to them to take cover under a rock, but the roar drowned out his wee voice. It was a distressing sight, but there was nothing he could do.

He noticed that, like him, many bees had taken cover outside the hive. He remembered what Bert had said about independent thinking beeing God's way of improving the species.

By now the storm was unleashing its full fury. The hail was so thick it obscured the hive. Driven by a fierce wind, it roared with an intensity that had the hair on Buzz's back standing on end. Just when he thought this was the most exciting thing he had ever seen, a bolt of lightning crashed not ten feet away, knocking Buzz on his rear.

Gradually the hail changed to rain and the wind slackened, leaving just a steady downpour. When Buzz was again able to see across the meadow, he looked for the hive, but it was gone.

Buzz wasn't surprised; this was by far the most violent storm he had ever seen. He was anxious to get to the hive and help, but the rain wouldn't permit it. Slowly it faded, turning into a steady drizzle. Still, Buzz forced himself to wait.

He began to feel chilly as he watched the water drip, drip, dripping off his boulder and splattering into the little pool it created at his feet. It was very quiet now and as he sat there, he thought of all the other bees scattered around the meadow, lost in the thoughts of their silent, solemn vigils. He wondered what he would find. How many survived? Did the queen make it? What would they do about the hive? There were big decisions to be made.

Finally the drizzle died almost completely and Buzz could wait no longer. He moved out from under his boulder, lifted off and headed for the hive. Many other bees were also emerging from their hiding places, flying stiffly in the cool, damp air. As he approached the hive, Buzz suddenly experienced the entire scene just as he had seen it in his dream! It was the hive he had seen on the ground, and all the bees were frantically circling it. Everything was covered with a layer of hail. It was uncanny!

The hive had two large tears in it. One exposed the honeycomb with their precious honey dripping onto the ground; the other revealed the fragile larvae beds. It was a sickening sight. Buzz wondered how many bees had been buried under the hail. Yet he had the strange sense that, despite the disaster, everything was unfolding exactly as it should.

Perfection isn't a state of affairs; it's a state of mind.

Panic and chaos had overcome the colony. No one seemed to know what to do. Most were automatically circling around and around, waiting for something to happen. Several others were digging through the rubble when suddenly one of them yelled, "The queen — she's alive!"

"THE QUEEN — SHE'S ALIVE!"

In an instant, several drones converged on the spot and helped pull the queen to safety. She appeared disoriented and disheveled, but otherwise unharmed. Everyone breathed a sigh of relief.

As word of the queen's survival spread among the colony, morale improved dramatically. Everyone seemed to instantly regain their sense of purpose. Without the queen, their society was doomed. Now they again had a reason to live.

When she had regained her wits, the queen summoned the colony leaders to decide what to do next. Buzz stood nearby, listening to the conversation. It was clear they intended to rebuild the hive exactly where it had been. Buzz was surprised at his reaction — he was disappointed, but at the same time felt no need to intervene. Again he had the uncanny sense that it was all perfect.

Just then the sun came out. The queen stopped midway through a sentence and rubbed her antennae together.

"Didn't someone once tell me there was a bee who said we should rebuild the hive in a safer place to avoid Boris?"

"Yes," one of the elders responded, "but he was...."

The queen interrupted him: "I think that's an excellent idea! Especially now that we've got to rebuild it anyway. Let's find a place safe not only from Boris, but from hailstorms as well."

We're all each other's students and teachers.

The elders all nodded their heads in agreement, congratulating the queen on her astute judgement.

That same afternoon the colony busily began rebuilding the hive in a large crack in a nearby cliff. It was further from the meadow, but it was as safe as a hive could get.

It was mid-morning before Buzz was first recognized. "Hey, aren't you the bee who disappeared earlier this summer?"

"That's right."

"Well I'll be darned. We all thought you were dead. Where have you been?"

"Oh, I just went off to see some new country."

By that time several bees had congregated around Buzz, curious and amazed that anyone could be gone that long from his hive. But not one asked about what he had encountered. It was just as well, Buzz thought.

Work progressed rapidly, and within two weeks the new hive was complete. The entire colony worked the hardest they had ever worked, and by the time the hive was finished everyone was totally exhausted.

The next day, it was work as usual. As he was flying to the meadow, Buzz overheard one young bee complaining to some elders, "We've just spent two weeks working the hardest we've ever worked in our lives. We need a little break. What's the point of this continuous de-beeizing work if we can't relax every once in a while and enjoy ourselves?"

"The point, young bee, is that we build upon our standard of living and create a better life for our young ones."

"But I am a young one, and I can tell you, this life you've created isn't worth living. I see no happiness on your faces. Why do you want to foist this on us?"

"No happiness? Why I'm, I'm very happy," the older bee scowled.

The younger bee could see it was hopeless. He flew off, meandered deep into the woods and landed on a fallen log.

Buzz smiled and followed, quietly landing nearby. The younger bee looked up, dejected. Buzz smiled reassuringly. "I saw what happened back there....felt like you could probably use a little encouragement."

There are no messiahs or saviors; only masters and teachers.